Introduction

"Quit going into my room!"

"I didn't go in your room!"

"Did so!"

Does this sound familiar? Stop this invasion of privacy once and for all. With your very own door alarm, you'll know the second someone opens your door. The prowler who trips your alarm will face a red light and a high-pitched shrill.

With this kit, as you assemble your own door alarm, you will discover the ins and outs of electricity and the electrical components that make your door alarm tick. Let's get going so you can install your door alarm and put it to work!

Warning #1: Do not use any source of electricity other than a 9-volt battery with your door alarm. The current from wall sockets or appliances is very, very strong and can cause you great injury.

Warning #2: Do not connect the two terminals of the battery directly together with a component or other metal. The battery and wire will generate enough heat to burn you!

1

What Is Electricity, Anyway?

A day doesn't go by that you don't use electricity. But what is it? You can't see it, so how do you know it's there? Electricity is the invisible fuel that runs lots of things in our lives. Look around you. There are probably many things in your room that are powered by electricity. Count them: lights, clocks, computer, TV, radio, the door (okay, probably not the door, but it *will* be once you hook up your alarm).

It all starts with atoms, the tiny invisible building blocks that make up everything. I mean *everything!*

Atoms have even smaller parts called electrons. There are times when one atom will pass an electron to another atom. These electrons, each of which has a tiny electric charge, are so small that more than one hundred million of them lined up wouldn't make it across the period at the end of this sentence.

Insulators and Conductors: The Stop and Go of Electric Flow

Materials that electricity can flow through are called *conductors*. Many metals, such as copper, aluminum, iron, and gold, are good electrical conductors. Atoms in conductors pass electrons to one another.

Insulators, like plastic, rubber, and glass, are poor conductors. They have atoms that hold on to their electrons and don't pass them along. These stable atoms have no room to hold new electrons, and they have no extra electrons to "throw." This blocks electrons from flowing. In your door alarm, the electrical insulator (the colored plastic coating) is used to cover conductors such as the metal wires.

So Just What Is Electricity?

I was getting to that! Electricity occurs when lots of electrons move in the same direction. And you've got electricity when you've completed a circuit. That's when the wires touch and your door alarm buzzes. And talk about fast, the movement of electricity happens close to the speed of light— that's 186,000 miles (300,000 km) per second! That's fast.

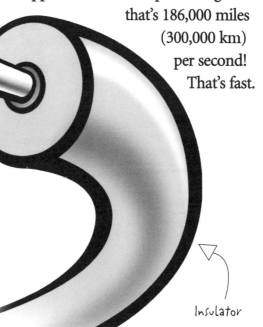

Conductor

Insulator

3

Fold the Box

Now let's get started. First you need to assemble the alarm box so all the other parts have a place to hang out.

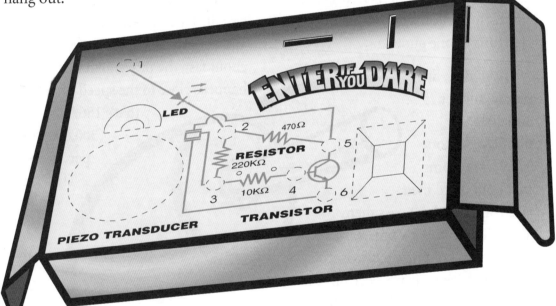

Assembly Instructions

Fold up box and tuck in flaps at both ends.

Spring!

No, not flowers, birds, and sunshine. These springs are the coils of wire that will hold the components in place in your door alarm. The springs are just the right size to fit into the large holes punched in the top of the cardboard box you just assembled. If the holes aren't punched all the way through, take a pencil and push the extra cardboard through the hole. Then push a spring about halfway into holes 2, 3, 4, 5, and 6, not hole 1! Put the smaller end of the springs into the holes. You should have two springs left over.

You are now ready to begin installing your components, but first these words of warning: Some of these parts will not work or will get permanently zapped if they are not put in the right way. Pay close attention to the directions, or you'll be trotting down to your local electronics supply store for replacement parts.

Resistor

Assembly Instructions

Gold/Silver
Brown
Purple
Yellow

The first components to hook up are the *resistors*. Find the 470-ohm resistor (its stripes are yellow, purple, and brown) and connect one end to spring 2 by bending the spring, placing the end of the wire in the spring, and releasing the spring. Then connect the other end of the resistor to spring 5. Next, find the 220K-ohm resistor (red, red, yellow, and gold) and connect it to springs 2 and 3. Use a different slot in the spring for each wire you attach to a spring. Finally, connect the 10K-ohm resistor (brown, black, orange, and gold) to springs 3 and 4.

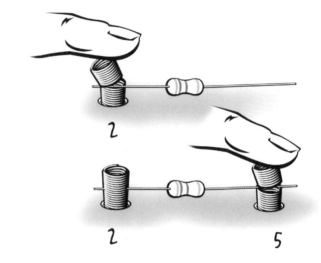

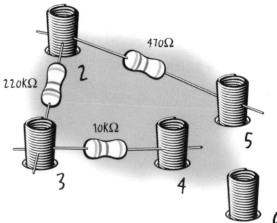

What's Happening

Resistors, as the name implies, resist the flow of electrons. They are used to control how much electricity is traveling in a circuit, which is often important.

Carbon, which is inside resistors, is a bad conductor. This means that carbon doesn't conduct electricity very well, so only a small amount of electricity can flow through it. Resistors with different amounts of carbon inside can be used to allow different amounts of electricity to flow in a circuit.

The other components in your door alarm need only a small amount of electricity. The battery produces more electricity than these components need, and without resistors they'd get fried!

The striped plastic coating on the resistors is not just for decoration. The colors are a code system that tells you just how much resistance each is willing (or able) to give. This resistance is measured in a unit called *ohms,* named for (what a surprise!) Georg Simon Ohm.

Connecting the Transistor

Assembly Instructions

Connect the transistor to springs 4, 5, and 6. The rounded side of the transistor must face to the left! The top lead wire goes to spring 5. The middle wire goes to spring 4, and the bottom wire goes to spring 6. It is very important that the wires are in the right springs!

Transistors are the most common of all semiconductors. As you already know, conductors let electrons flow easily, and insulators don't let them flow at all. So a semiconductor is halfway in between. It is a conductor when electricity is flowing in the right direction and an insulator when electricity is flowing in the wrong direction. That's why it's so important to connect the right wires into the right springs. Transistors are found in most modern electronics, from stereos to computers to digital watches, and now they are in door alarms!

You know that resistors can control the flow of electricity, but they cannot vary the flow. With a transistor you can change the amount of electricity that is allowed to flow.

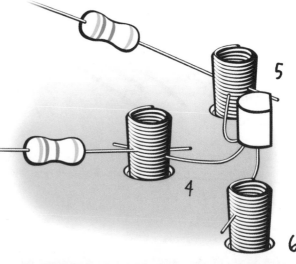

What's Happening

A transistor works like a small electricity valve, similar to a garden hose valve that turns water on and off. The top leg, the *collector*, is where electricity comes in. The bottom leg, the *emitter*, is where electricity goes out. The middle leg, the *base*, turns the flow on and off. If just a little bit of electricity comes into the base, it will open the transistor and let a lot of electricity flow from the collector to the emitter. If the middle leg doesn't get any electricity, then no electricity goes through. Sometimes a transistor is called an amplifier because it increases the size of an electrical signal.

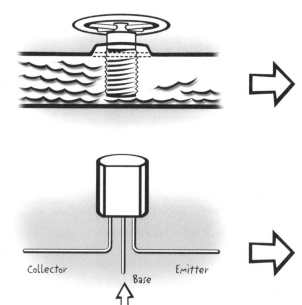

Connecting the Piezo Transducer

Assembly Instructions

Fold up the tab on the box to hold the *piezo transducer* in place. It's that round disk with the metal inside. Thread all the wires through the hole, starting from underneath the tab as shown. Connect the red wire to spring 5, the orange wire to spring 3, and the black wire to spring 6.

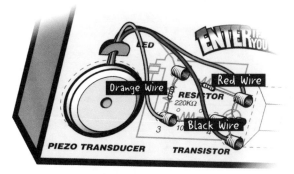

PIEZO TRANSDUCER — Orange Wire — Red Wire — RESISTOR 220KΩ — Black Wire — TRANSISTOR — LED — ENTER

Make Some Noise

The piezo transducer makes noise — lots of loud, high-pitched noise —

when electricity goes through it. *Piezo* (pronounced pee-AY-zoh) is Greek for pressure. A *transducer* is something that can change one kind of energy into another.

The metal disk inside this transducer expands and contracts as pressure is put on it by electricity passing through it. So a piezo transducer, kind of like a simple stereo speaker, changes electricity into sound waves.

What's Happening

The piezo electric disk expands when electricity flows through it and contracts when the electricity stops. When the electricity *oscillates* — turns on and off and on and off repeatedly — the disk bends out and in and out and in, which creates sound waves.

Connecting the LED

Assembly Instructions

Connect the LED to springs 1 and 2. The LED is the red plastic bulb with the wires sticking out. It is *very important* that the shorter wire on the LED is connected to spring 2! The flat edge of the LED should be toward spring 2.

Flat Edge

1

2

You just installed your Light Emitting Diode, or "LED" for short. *Diodes* are one-way valves for electricity.

What's Happening

LEDs are special diodes because they give off light when electricity passes through them. Because they are diodes, they only let electricity flow in one direction. Hold your LED up to the light. That metal you see inside is called a "semiconductor junction." This is the part that allows the electrical current to flow in only one direction. LEDs are used in computers, stereos, televisions, video games, calculators, alarm clocks, VCRs, and many other electronic gizmos. On your door-alarm board, the LED is being used to flash a warning of an impending break-in.

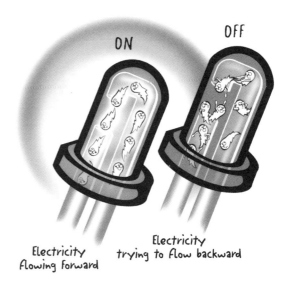

ON

OFF

Electricity
Flowing Forward

Electricity
trying to Flow backward

Assemble the Plastic Piece

Assembly Instructions

Now it's time to put the plastic piece on your door alarm. This is a little tricky, but you only have to do it once!

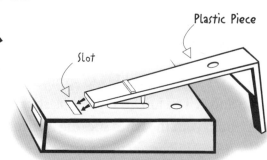

Carefully slide the end of the plastic piece into the slot on top of the door alarm.

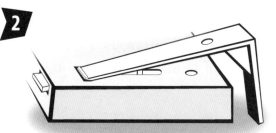

Gently push the end of the piece through the slot at the edge of the box. It should snap in place.

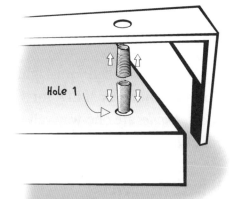

Place a spring through the hole in the plastic piece, from underneath. Then place another spring into hole 1 in the box.

Battery

Assembly Instructions

Connect the red wire on the battery connector to the spring on the plastic piece. Connect the black wire on the connector to spring 6. Place a 9-volt battery in the rectangular hole as shown and connect the battery connector to the battery. When the battery is hooked up, test to see if

your alarm sounds and if the light is working. Double check the LED connection, because if it's backward, nothing is going to work.

Yeow! Okay, disconnect it! I told you it was a loud noise.

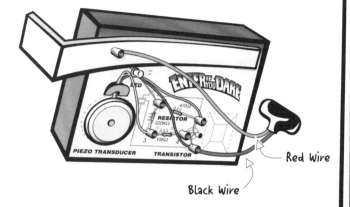

Red Wire

Black Wire

What's Happening

The *battery* supplies the power to pump the electrons through the wire. The battery passes electrons out of the negative terminal to the first atom at the beginning of the loop of wire, which passes electrons down the line. The last atom in the wire passes an electron to the positive terminal. The battery picks up the electron and puts it back into circulation in the battery.

Installing Your Alarm

Installation Instructions

Let's try out the alarm on your door. First, turn the alarm off by disconnecting the red wire from the spring on the plastic piece. Using strips of double-stick tape, connect the door alarm to your door as shown. Before you peel off the double-stick tape, try holding the alarm on your door and open and close the door to make sure you've got it in the right position. It's hard to move the alarm once you put it on the door. When the door is closed, the plastic piece should bend up, so that the two springs no longer touch. This breaks the electrical circuit and turns off the sound and light. When your door opens, the springs touch and the alarm goes off! Reconnect the red wire as you leave and see who becomes the first to fall into your trap!

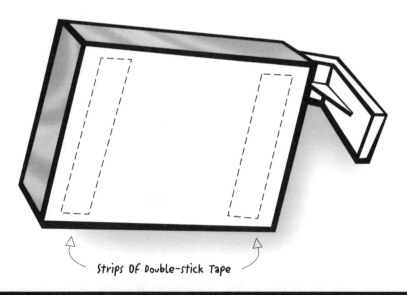

Strips Of Double-stick Tape

Door closed,
alarm off.

Door opened,
alarm on.

Troubleshooting

Okay, so you've got your alarm all connected and…nothing happens. Before you take the whole thing apart, recheck all the connections. Is there only metal touching metal? Make sure no plastic is pinched in the springs. Still nothing? Check the battery. If the battery is okay, try these two tests to determine whether your LED and transistor are still working:

Test #1: The LED

Pull all the components off—we're going for a clean start. Connect the LED to springs 1 and 2. Remember, the flat edge goes toward spring 2. The 470-ohm resistor (yellow, purple, brown, and gold) goes into 2 and 5. The black battery wire goes to 5, and the red wire goes into 1. Connect the battery and the LED should light up. If it doesn't, make sure the flat edge of the LED is toward spring 2.

Test #2: The Piezo Transducer

If the wires on the piezo transducer are pulled tight, it may not make any noise. Gently pull on the piezo disk so that it is loosely hanging by its wires. Turn on the alarm, and gently move the piezo disk to get the loudest sound.

Test #3: The Transistor

Transistors are very delicate. To make sure yours isn't burned out, hook up the whole circuit from the beginning. Once you've connected it, remove the piezo transducer. Connect the battery, and the LED should light.

If it doesn't, the transistor is fried. Go to your local electronics supply store (like Radio Shack) and get a general purpose NPN transistor, such as a 2N3904 (Radio Shack part 276-2009 or 276-2016). They're pretty cheap, so it won't blow your allowance.